WILD
FAMILY

Written by
Ben Lerwill

Illustrated by
Harriet Hobday

PUFFIN

What does the word 'FAMILY' mean to you?

It might mean something different to each and every one of us. As humans, our families come in every possible shape and size.

Nature, too, has many kinds of different families. Some animals have thousands of babies. Some have just one or two. Some spend their whole lives in packs, herds, flocks or colonies. Some roam solo. In this book, we'll explore some of the most fascinating families in the natural world. We'll travel to towering rainforests, frozen plains, tropical seas and dark caves. We'll find out what makes human families similar to those of other creatures . . . and what makes us different, too.

Of course, that's not all – every living thing on Earth also has something vitally important in common: we share a home. We share the winds that blow, the plants that grow and the rivers that flow. We share a magical, carefully balanced planet brimming with biodiversity.

And we're all members of another family. Every single thing that lives here is part of the same tree of life, which means that all of us belong to one giant family – one far bigger than a single species. And in this family, every living thing matters.

Every insect, every fish,
every tree, every bird.
Everything that grows, flies,
creeps, swims and climbs.
Because here on Earth . . . we are

ONE WILD FAMILY.

One planet.
Seven continents.
Five oceans.
Millions of species.

We'll discover the stories of some of these species . . .

. . . and see how we're part of ONE **WILD** FAMILY.

What is . . . *a wild family?*

For scientists, an animal family means something very specific: a group of creatures that share certain features. For example, tigers, lions and jaguars are all members of the cat family.

But in this book, we'll look at wild families in a different way. We'll explore how different species look after their babies and protect each other. We'll discover how some of these animal families live in tight groups, working together to find food and stay safe. We'll also find out how some have learned clever ways of surviving alongside other species.

A wild family can be many things.

It can be a **school of fish** or a **nest of ants**.

It can even be a **group of humans** – just like you and the people you live with.

What is . . . biodiversity?

Millions of species shape our world. Worms, wolves, whales and waterlilies. Leopards, lizards, llamas and lobsters. Holly trees, hedgehogs, hummingbirds and hippos. Think about that for a moment. Millions of species.

What a miracle! What a place!

How extraordinary to be living in such a rich web of life!

But here's the most magical thing of all:

Every single species has a role to play in how our planet works. Biodiversity means 'the variety of life on Earth'. It's the way in which every living thing is connected to every other living thing. It's what makes our world the place it is.

As humans, we need countless other animals and plants just to keep us alive, from the bees that pollinate our crops to the forests and ocean algae that give us oxygen. We're one piece in the great jigsaw of life – and without the other pieces we'd be in serious trouble.

All life on our fragile planet needs biodiversity to help it survive. The natural world is a giant family tree – that we're all a part of.

So let's meet some of our *wild family* . . .

A swaying HERD of ELEPHANTS: giants on the march . . .

With a slow-motion roll and rumble, a family of elephants moves through the African dawn. They walk in single file on tree-trunk legs, swishing their fly-swatter tails. At the front of the group is the matriarch: the female leader. She is usually the oldest and largest female in the family. The matriarch decides where the herd goes and what it does. Plodding patiently behind are her sisters, daughters and all their children. Male elephants, known as bulls, stay with the herd until they're around ten years old and then they tend to roam solo.

Elephants have heads as big as boulders, with brains to match.

They are some of the most intelligent creatures in the world, and have jumbo memory spans. Older members of a family group are able to remember where they found food and water decades earlier. And young calves learn from their elders, such as how to grip fallen branches with their trunks and scratch their own backs.

An elephant family is a faithful one. The animals travel, socialize and forage together – a team of hefty herbivores tearing leaves from the trees. The females even babysit for each other. Calves are looked after not just by their mothers but also by other adult females in the herd, and it's even common for calves to suckle milk from more than one female.

Elephants can show kindness to other species, too: there are stories of them protecting dogs, baby rhinos – and even humans.

Elephants have the longest **gestation** period of any mammal, carrying their young for 18 to 22 months before giving birth. This long pregnancy gives plenty of time for an unborn calf to develop the brain power it needs to survive when it's born.

Another thing that makes elephants so extraordinary is the way they act when a member of their family dies. They often gather silently around the bones of a dead relative, as though paying their respects. Sometimes they stand guard for hours, or even days, laying branches on the body or touching it with their trunks. Elephants from other families might even come and mourn with them.

Just as we grieve for the people we were close to, elephants mourn, too.

An elephant's trunk has 40,000 muscles . . .

but there are still parts of its body that it can't reach. That's why it's happy for this flock of **oxpeckers** to perch on its back. The small birds use their red beaks to pick **flies**, **ticks** and **maggots** from the elephant's skin – and they do the same job for **buffaloes**, **rhinos** and **hippos**. The birds even hiss loudly when they see danger approaching . . . so they're not just bug-cleaners, but warning alarms, too.

As the world's largest land mammals, elephants are fantastically strong. They also have their own personalities – scientists have discovered that within a herd, there are four main characters: natural leaders, playful scamps, gentle giants and general helpers.

Which one would you be?

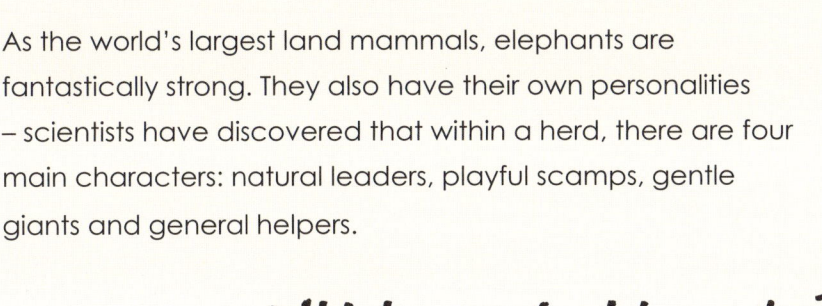

Elephants are what is known as a **keystone species**. This means they play an essential role in their environment and help the biodiversity of the African plains. They use their trunks and curved tusks to dig up dry riverbeds, which brings water to the surface for them, and other animals, to drink. And because they chomp on trees and shrubs, they help keep the plains open for families of **zebras** and **antelopes**.

And one more thing. It's brown. It's mucky.

It's a football-sized lump of fresh elephant dung . . . but it's also a buffet for creepy-crawlies! Elephants don't digest all their food, so **millipedes**, **crickets** and **termites** can all find things to feed on here. **Dung beetles** roll elephant poo into balls to save as a tasty snack and as a warm place to lay their eggs in. All this insect activity attracts other animals, too, so **honey badgers** and **hornbills** often arrive to root through the dung for an insect meal of their own.

A flutter of BUTTERFLIES
on whispering wings . . .

This confetti-burst of colour is a sky full of **monarch butterflies**. It's late summer, and the insects are on a long, flip-flapping journey from the woods of the USA and Canada to the warm mountains of Mexico. In many months, when winter's over, they'll fly north again . . .

When animals make mighty journeys like this, we call it **migration**. Migrating animals travel to find the conditions that are best for them. As they journey through different regions, they help new habitats become even more biodiverse. Monarchs pollinate plants and flowers as they go, and even provide a source of food for some birds, disappearing into their butterfly-gobbling beaks.

When these tiny butterflies migrate, they roost for the night with other monarchs, clustering together on tree branches. Together, these little orange aeronauts can stay warm and safe.

This family tale will set your mind aflutter.

On their way back north in early spring, the butterflies lay their eggs, dying soon after. Their children continue the journey, living for just a few weeks before laying eggs and dying too. This cycle continues throughout the migration. Amazingly, the butterflies that fly south to Mexico the next summer are the great-grandchildren of the insects that made the same journey the year before! Monarchs need many generations of their family to complete each epic annual journey.

Biodiversity sometimes produces very specific partnerships. Monarch butterflies can skip through the skies to find different plants to feed on – but their caterpillars are much fussier. They eat only **milkweed plants**, so without milkweed, we'd have no monarchs.

Female monarch butterflies lay hundreds of tiny eggs in their short lifetimes.

They grow into stripy,

hairy caterpillars, which soon turn into

butterflies, and the cycle begins again . . .

A shimmering School of CLOWNFISH . . .

Swimming through shafts of sunlight in the warm seas of Australia are these rainbow-bright **clownfish**. They might be small, but they're excellent egg-parents. The mother lays hundreds at a time, which are guarded closely by the father. Both the mother and father make sure the eggs get lots of care and protection. But when they hatch around ten days later, the parents' job is over – and the tiny clownfish drift away by themselves to start new lives in the tropical waters.

It's easy to see how clownfish get their name – their bold bright stripes look like a clown's face-paint. They're also known as **clown anemonefish**, which is a bit of a mouthful, but it hints at the amazing relationship they have with a wavy animal that lives on the seafloor . . .

A clownfish family is a very unusual one.

A group is usually made up of a female, a male and several **neuter** clownfish – neuter means they're neither male nor female. But if the female dies, then one of the neuter clownfish will become female to take her place.

The sea is full of underwater biodiversity - almost a quarter of a million known species live in the world's oceans!

Although they look like plants, sea anemones are animals – and their floaty tentacles are poisonous. Clownfish have a special coating on their skin that stops them from being stung, but other fish aren't so lucky.

. . . clownfish like to live inside sea **anemones**, to protect themselves from predators. But that's not all. The fish clean pests from the anemones' tentacles and also drop meal scraps, giving the anemones more food – so the anemones are happy with their house guests, too.

A PRIDE of LIONS, prowling the plains . . .

A royal roar echoes over the land. **Lions** are the kings and queens of the African grasslands, padding across the open plains on golden paws. Speed, strength and sharp-clawed teamwork put this powerful family at the very top of the food chain.

Most of the pride are quick-thinking females, although the big boss is usually a shaggy-maned male. Energetic **cubs**, and often one or two young males, make up the rest of the group. When young males become adults they usually leave their family behind, searching the savannah for a **pride** of their own to rule . . .

Can you imagine being licked by a long, scratchy lion tongue? That's exactly how lions keep each other's coats clean.

As muscular **meat-eaters**, lions have a vital role in the biodiversity of the savannah. The land can be grazed bare if there are too many grass-chomping **antelopes** and **zebras**, so by hunting the weakest and slowest animals, lions are keeping the **herbivore** population at a healthy level – and their own bellies full.

Lions might be deadly, but they also have enemies.

These spotted hyenas often try to snatch food that lions have caught. A pack of snarling hyenas isn't easy to fight. Lions and hyenas both scavenge each other's kills, which means this lively rivalry can sometimes benefit them both.

Lions keep low while stalking prey. The long pale grass helps them hunt by camouflaging their light-brown coats. When they catch a meal, the pride takes it in turns to feed.

A teeming COLONY of TERMITES...

Meet the miniature military, working tirelessly in the evening heat. This tall mound looks like a tree stump – but it's actually a nest made by millions of **termites**. The insects build up their family fortress by using soil, spit and their own poo, then work all day to protect it. Some African termite mounds are taller than a person!

All these termites have the same mother. The **queen** is much bigger than the other termites and lives in a dark chamber deep inside the nest – she can lay an egg every three seconds! Over her lifetime, she'll have millions of children. Other termites group around the queen, protecting, feeding and cleaning her.

One reason for having such a large family is the danger of being eaten. Animals such as **aardvarks** feed on ants and termites – one aardvark can slurp up tens of thousands of termites in a single night!

Termites are nature's master builders. A **termite mound** is full of tunnels, with special chimneys to help air flow in and out.

All the termites in the **colony** have their own jobs.

Some are eager **workers**, collecting food and repairing the mound when it gets damaged. Others are strong-jawed **soldiers**, defending their home from invaders.

These swarming attackers are **Matabele ants**. They have a nest of their own, but right now they're on a mission to munch on termites. Matabele ants are quick and dangerous – but they're also excellent paramedics. If one of the group gets injured during a raid, its comrades carry it carefully back to the nest, where it can recover. Injured ants even have their wounds cared for by their nest-mates.

The bustling buzz of a SWARM of BEES . . .

Bees have been buzzing around since the age of the dinosaurs, around 100 million years ago. They're still some of the most important animals on the planet. The work they do – for each other and for the world – is a miracle we all rely on.

A **beehive** contains tens of thousands of bees, all of which come from eggs laid by the tireless **queen bee**. Every insect in the hive has a job to do – and the queen's task is to make more bees. It's one big, buzzing family!

A hive is a bit like a big maternity ward.

The queen lays one egg in each **honeycomb** cell. When the eggs hatch, small white **larvae** emerge. They're bee babies!

The other female bees are known as **worker bees**. They never stop. Worker bees keep the honeycomb cells clean and look after the wriggling larvae. They also fly outside on special missions to collect **pollen** and **nectar** to feed the colony.

Bees speak by dancing! They waggle, hop and turn in circles to tell other bees in the hive where to find pollen and nectar.

Male bees are called **drones**. They have one main purpose in life, which is to mate with the queen. This means that although the bees in the hive all have the same mother, there are lots of different fathers.

When the hive gets too hot, this big family works together to keep each other cool. Some fan their wings and others fly out to fill their tummies with water. Back at the hive, they spit it out for other bees to share.

Bees work as a team to make **honey**. When one bee brings nectar to the hive, other bees chew it, then dry it and store it. Soon it becomes sticky honey. Bees don't do this so that we have something to put on our toast, but so that they have something to eat during the colder winter months. Honey is full of energy, which is exactly what this busy, buzzy family needs.

Blazing reds, violent pinks, dazzling yellows. One of the reasons flowers are so colourful and sweet-smelling is to attract insects to help pollinate them.

A single honey bee is almost as light as air . . . but the job it does for the world is a mammoth one. All flowering plants need to be pollinated to reproduce. Some plants can do this by themselves, but many need insects to help them to produce seeds. And there's no better-known pollinator than a bee.

To a honey bee, a brightly petalled flower means a drink of sugary nectar. But here's the clever part: when the bee crawls inside the flower to slurp up the nectar, tiny pollen grains stick to its legs and body. At the next flower the bee visits, some of these grains fall off – and this new flower is pollinated.

Bees and other pollinators are a vital part of life on Earth. They help the environment, just as the environment helps them.

Insect pollination is an essential part of the planet's biodiversity. Without it, many of the plants we eat wouldn't be able to make fruit or reproduce. Fruits like **apples**, **blackberries**, **plums**, **pears** and **mangoes** would disappear, and so would things like **carrots**, **onions**, **broccoli** and **leeks**. Even chocolate comes from a plant that needs to be pollinated!

A wide-eyed bunch of DEER

We're in the scorching wilds of northern India. Smell the earthy warmth of the gnarled trees and the sun-bleached meadows. Can you see the **deer** browsing the grass and hear the **grey langur monkeys** jostling in the branches? But wait. Far off in the shadows, there's something else astir . . .

In the distance – a **tiger!** She's left her young cubs hidden in the bushes while she goes hunting.

These patterned beauties are **chitals**, or **spotted deer**. By sticking together in herds while they feed, they have more pairs of eyes to spot danger.

...and a barking troop of MONKEYS

The monkeys and the deer have a very special relationship – they act as lookouts for each other. If a deer sees a predator approaching, it makes a high barking noise. If a monkey spots it first, it makes a loud alarm call of its own. Then both species react to the danger.

The deer have another reason for staying close to the langurs. Monkeys often drop fruit and foliage from the trees – which means extra snacks for the deer. And can you see the black birds waiting close by? They're **common mynas**, and they're here to feed on the insects disturbed by the grazing deer. Monkeys, deer and myna birds are three very different families – but they've learned the benefits of living together.

A SLEUTH of PANDAS, crunching bamboo . . . .

In the high mountains of China live bears as black as night and as white as snow. This **giant panda** and her **cubs** are doing what they love best: eating! Adult females like this mother can eat for up to 12 hours a day, chewing on a leafy plant called **bamboo.**

These two cubs will stay close to their mum for the first year and a half of their lives. She teaches them the tricks of being a perfect panda, from climbing trees to finding bamboo. The baby bears are pink and tiny when they're born but they soon grow big enough to have roly-poly play-fights.

Bamboo makes up a whopping 99% of a giant panda's food. China has more than 500 species of this hollow, fast-growing plant, but without a steady supply, it's impossible for a panda to stay fat and strong.

Not all animals live in big family groups. Giant pandas are usually private and solitary creatures, plodding leisurely around the forests. Their lives are peaceful because they have very few natural predators, and they help the forest by spreading plant seeds in their droppings. Smelly? Yes. But it's great for the vegetation!

But what's this flash of colour down here?

It's a pair of **red pandas**. Male and female red pandas only meet in the green warmth of spring, when they need to mate. Sniffing the thick woodland with their wide, black noses, they use their outstanding sense of smell to find each other.

Red pandas nest in trees, and their cubs stay in the nest for three whole months. They love bamboo too, but just like their distant cousins, the giant pandas, their future is at risk from **deforestation**.

Look closely at those vine-grabbing hands and shell-like ears. These magnificent **chimpanzees** have more in common with us than any other creature in the world. All living things contain something called DNA, which is nature's recipe for how that thing looks, grows and behaves. The DNA of chimpanzees and humans is about 98% the same, making them our closest living relatives.

So let's meet the family . . .

A troop of CHIMPANZEES, the forest acrobats . . .

Tropical trees provide the perfect habitat for chimpanzees. They use leaves and branches to build bed-nests each night, and younger chimps learn how to do this by watching their relatives.

Chimpanzees live in the tropical forests of central and western Africa. Just like us, they're sociable animals. A troop of chimps is a giant gang of up to 150 males, females and babies. They climb, play, shriek, snooze, squabble and eat together. They wrestle when they're fidgety and bum-scratch when they're itchy. But it's more than just a hairy chaos! Each troop has two main leaders, known as the alpha male and female. The alphas need to stay strong and healthy to avoid losing their position.

Baby chimps stay close to their mothers for many years, clinging on to their backs and drinking their milk.

When they need to, older brothers and sisters will help to care for the babies, too.

Chimps aren't always cute and cuddly. In the 1970s, a big troop of chimps in Tanzania's Gombe Stream National Park split into two groups and spent four years in a violent battle for power. Many were killed. But the animals can also show amazing kindness to each other. We know that if a chimpanzee has lost a fight, other chimps often come and play with them, or even hug them, to make them feel better.

Chimps can scamper up tree trunks far faster than any human. Such jungle gymnastics helps them reach one of their favourite fruits: **wild figs**. The figs grow high off the forest floor, but they wouldn't be there at all without the help of a special insect. Tiny **fig wasps** fly into unripe figs, which is the only place they can lay their eggs. They pollinate the fruit, but then die inside the fig straight afterwards. The wasps that hatch fly away to find other unripe figs, and the story repeats itself. So chimps eat figs, figs need fig wasps – and fig wasps need figs!

Has anyone ever brushed a minibeast off your back for you?

This is exactly what chimpanzees do for one another. They groom their friends and family by picking dirt, plants and insects from their hair.

Fishing rods and hammers aren't just human inventions. Chimpanzees have just as many fingers and thumbs as we do, and they've learned to make tools. In some troops they use long twigs to 'fish' in termite nests. Other troops use branches and stones as nutcrackers, placing the nuts on flat rocks then hammering them open. Some even use leaves and moss as spoons for drinking water.

Different troops learn different skills, and pass these down to their children.

Here in Gombe Stream National Park, these **African paradise flycatchers** are one of more than 200 bird species in this thick forest. The males and females build their nests together, using leaves, small roots, animal hair and even spiderwebs. They guard their eggs well, then take it in turns to fetch insects for the chicks when they're born, diving and turning to catch flies in mid-air.

From the tangled trees comes the chattering chorus of the JUNGLE FAMILY . . .

Many, many species call the **Amazon rainforest** home. Birds flit, monkeys chant, flowers bloom, insects buzz. The forest here teems with life, from its steamy pools to its sky-high treetops. This sweltering South American jungle is the largest in the world, with more types of plants and animals than anyone has ever been able to count. Rainforests like the Amazon have dizzyingly high levels of biodiversity.

These dazzling sparks of colour are **poison dart frogs**. Each one is no bigger than a toothbrush head but contains enough venom to kill ten people. And what do two of them have on their backs? Tadpoles! Fathers carry their babies around the jungle to find water for them to grow in.

Meet the go-slow family. **Three-toed sloths** spend almost all their lives in the trees, sleeping for up to 20 hours a day. This baby will stay close to its mother for at least five months, using its little claws to cling on to her fur.

This dark tree hollow was made by a **woodpecker** – but now it's a nest for a clutch of **toucan** chicks. Their banana-beaked parents take it in turns to keep the eggs warm and to feed the chicks with wild fruit when they're hatched. The chicks stay in the nest for six to eight weeks, then flap away into the jungle to look after themselves.

A female **wolf spider** creeps along a log, with a ball of crawling spiderlings on her back. For the past few weeks, she's been carrying a silken sac of eggs under her abdomen.

Eight legs, eight eyes, 100 babies

After hatching, the young spiders climb on to their mother's back to keep safe. They'll stay here for days, then scuttle their separate ways . . .

Welcome to the underworld, where the sun never shines and the breeze never blows. **Soil** sticks to our shoes and gets under our fingernails, but it's also one of the most important things in the world. The soil below our feet is a hidden superstore full of water, nutrients and carbon. And as well as being a vital ingredient for life on our planet, it's also a home for endless families of **creepy-crawlies** . . .

A SWARM
of soil-dwellers . . .

Soil is absolutely swarming with living things, from **ants** and **mites** to **fungi** and **bacteria**. Many of them are far too small for us to see – one tiny pinch of soil can contain a billion bacteria! **We can think of soil as the world's stomach.** The things that live here eat, digest and recycle loads of crucial nutrients and organisms – helping new life to grow.

The long slithering creature below is a **caecilian**. It looks like a cross between a snake and a worm, although it's actually a legless amphibian. Experts think caecilians have lived on Earth for around 100 million years. Here in South America, they spend most of their time in the soil and often dig underground to lay their eggs. When their babies are born, something very strange happens. The mother feeds her children by letting them chew off a layer of her own skin. And when they're full? She grows the skin back for their next meal!

Earthworms have no ears, eyes, nose or teeth . . . but scientists have discovered that some worms use touch to communicate with each other and can decide as a group which way to squirm!

These **northern white rhinos** are majestic beasts. They might be gentle plant-eaters but they're as strong as tanks, with heads like rocks and hides like dinosaur skin. For countless years they've lived in family groups, rumbling across the grassy plains of East Africa. Their excellent sense of smell helps them find other rhinos, and their hefty horns come in handy when females need to protect their calves. But today they have a problem. A rhino-sized one.

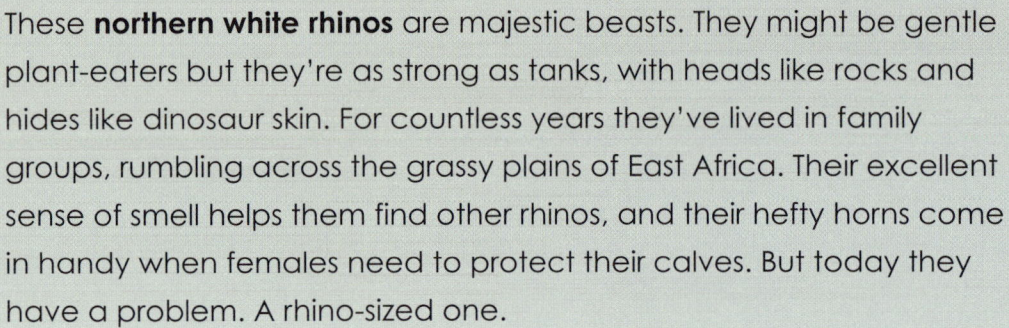

Rumbling across the land, a **CRASH** of RHINOS ... and then silence

There are just two adult northern white rhinos left anywhere in the world: a mother and daughter named **Najin** and **Fatu**. They live on a wildlife reserve in Kenya, where guards keep them safe. Scientists are trying different ways of helping them to have calves – but the future of the species is very much at risk.

Rhinos of different kinds have roamed this planet for tens of millions of years. Like so many species, these northern white rhinos have played an enormous part in the great web of life on the planet. If we lose them, it's forever – we'll never get them back.

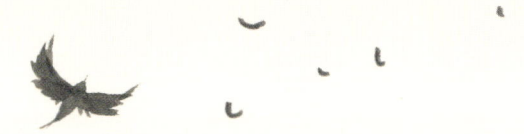

Many rhinos have been killed for their horns because of the false belief they can be used as a kind of medicine. **Poaching** is just one of the dangers wild animals face.

Unless we're careful, the sad story of these northern white rhinos might become a common one. Many of our species are at risk of extinction, from **orangutans** and **hawksbill turtles** to **polar bears** and **river dolphins**. It's our job to do everything we can to make sure this doesn't happen.

A flock of SEABIRDS, a clifftop kingdom . . .

This crowded cliff is home to one of nature's great spectacles: a super-sized **nesting colony**. It's perfect for the birds of the North Atlantic, who return to places like this each year to breed. Having so many feathered friends around helps protect them all from larger predators – in this way, these family groups can help each other.

Cliffs like this were formed naturally, but they make ideal nesting sites for seabirds.

Fulmars make their nests high up on the cliff-face. They have a special trick if intruders come too near – they squirt out stinky stomach oils from their beaks!

Further down the cliff, **gannets** create big, messy nests from grass and mud. When they go fishing to find food for their chicks, they dive into the ocean like missiles.

Can you spot the fast-moving **house martins**? They're here to catch flying insects that feed on nutrients in the seabird poo!

These nesting birds have learned how to share the colony to protect their seabird families – but they still need to be careful. **Black-backed gulls** patrol the cliff-face, looking for any unguarded eggs or chicks. Adult seabirds have developed lots of tricks to keep their newborns well shielded.

Guillemots squash together quietly on steep, rocky ledges. Each bird keeps its egg safe between its legs. By filling the ledge with their bodies, they give predators nowhere to land.

39

A wave-jumping School of DOLPHINS...

Speeding through the Atlantic Ocean comes a family of **bottlenose dolphins**. These marine mammals usually travel in pods of between 10 and 15, but sometimes cluster into enormous 'super-pods' of more than 1,000 dolphins! Unlike many other animals, they don't always stay in the same group, and sometimes switch pods to suit themselves. They've even been known to team up with other types of dolphin.

One of the most common arrangement of pods is made up of a mother and her calves. It's like a fast-swimming underwater playgroup.

Dolphins make different sounds to communicate with each other, letting them share life-saving messages. Ambush predators like **sharks** can easily catch a lone dolphin, but it's not so simple when the shark has to deal with a twisting, turning pod.

Dolphins find their food by using something called **echolocation**. They make a series of clicking noises – the sound travels out then bounces back from whatever creature happens to be swimming nearby. This lets the dolphin work out exactly where its next meal is – and then there's no escaping the snapping jaws of a hungry bottlenose.

Dolphins might look like they're always smiling but they can be agressive, too. The males sometimes clash, chasing and biting each other, often to stop their rivals from pairing up with females.

There's always a meal to be found in an environment as biodiverse as an ocean. Dolphins eat everything from **catfish** and **mackerel** to **mullet** and **squid**. They bring an important balance to the ocean food chain, which ranges from tiny **plankton** to huge **blue whales**.

Wrap up warm. We're heading for the teeth-chattering cold of the far south. These noble **emperor penguins** live in freezing Antarctica, where only the toughest animals and plants can survive. The shivery temperatures are harsh enough to leave icicles on a human's nose, but this flippered family knows how to keep its chicks safe and snug . . .

Monarchs of the ice:
a **huddle** of PENGUINS . . .

The biting winter winds of Antarctica can be far too wild and strong for a solo penguin, but the colony stays safe together. This enormous penguin-huddle is made up of thousands of adults and chicks.

The penguins in the centre of the group are protected from the icy storm, sheltered and toasty in a snuggle of bodies. But emperors aren't selfish. The colony slowly shuffles and turns as it moves across the land, giving every penguin time to get warm in the middle of the huddle.

Some colonies have tens of thousands of emperor penguins.

These **brown skuas** are also sheltering from the icy storm. The birds are cunning hunters, and when the wind drops, they work in pairs to distract adult penguins and grab their chicks. This can seem cruel, but nature reminds us that skuas need to eat, too. Male and female skuas often pair for life, laying two eggs of their own each year.

Once a year, the female emperor penguin produces a single, fragile egg. As soon as it's laid, the male carefully scoops it into a pouch between his feet to keep it off the cold ice. For two long months he'll keep it warm, no matter how much the icy wind howls around them. He won't leave the egg, even to find food – his job is to stand and wait.

Emperor penguins are the largest of all penguin species – the adults are the same height as a six-year-old human child.

During this time, the female goes to sea to feed. She returns around nine weeks later – fattened up on fish and squid – to find . . .

But what does the hungry little chick eat? Well, both its parents are able to cough up gooey food from their bellies, which they pass into the beak of the hungry chick. It might sound disgusting to us . . . but it's delicious to this penguin chick.

. . . a newly hatched ball of grey fluff! The chick and its parents nuzzle up together, but this happy family reunion is brief. Soon it's the male's turn to trundle off to the ocean and fill his tummy.

Without the fish that live in the cold seas, the penguins wouldn't be able to raise their chicks.

Emperor penguins love eating **Antarctic silverfish**. They're the most common fish in the sea here, and they're also the favourite meal of **seals** and **whales**. This makes the fish a vital species for biodiversity.

Orcas, or killer whales, are one of the world's top sea predators. Despite their name, they're actually the world's largest species of dolphin. They have 50 dagger-sharp teeth, swim faster than many boats and are as heavy as elephants. They also live in tight-knit groups, so when you meet one orca, you meet the whole family . . .

Cruising the big blue, a POD of ORCAS . . .

Pods can contain dozens of orcas, but simpler family groups are made up of a mother, her adult children and her daughter's children.

The big wide ocean gives orcas the two things they need most: food and freedom.

Many orcas stay with their mothers for their whole lives. The fathers usually come from different pods – they don't look after their own babies, but they do help to care for the young orcas they share a pod with.

No matter where in the world they live, orcas are pack hunters. Some circle around **shoals of herring**, blowing bubbles to herd the fish into a ball before slapping their super-strong tails to stun them. And here in Antarctica, hunting orcas zoom side by side under ice floes where seals are resting, making wild waves that wash their whiskered prey into the water.

Crabeater seals have special tricks of their own. Their saw-like teeth act like a sieve, which lets them gobble up mouthfuls of krill without having to swallow seawater. Like other seals, they also prefer to do their own thing. Although they're sometimes spotted in colonies of up to 1,000, or swimming in giant herds, they usually spend most of their time alone or in small groups. Males and females often meet up only once a year to have a single **pup** in the spring.

There's nuffin' like a **puffin!** On land, these bright little seabirds waddle around outside their family burrows like fussy caretakers, but in seawater they zoom deep into the blue, seeking out tasty **sand eels**. And in the air? They whizz around like bullets, their wings beating six times a second!

A CIRCUS of PUFFINS zipping through the sky . . .

Puffins might be small, but they have big responsibilities. Males and females usually mate for life. After spending eight months of each year at sea – often many miles apart from each other – they both arrive back at their cosy clifftop burrow, where the female lays a single egg. When it hatches, the parents take it in turns to rocket into the waves to find eels and fish for the chick to eat. The chicks are called **pufflings**.

When they meet up at their burrow every spring, the males and females spend time rubbing their stripy bills together. They usually haven't seen each other for a long time – so this charming beak-to-beak ritual is a way of keeping their relationship strong.

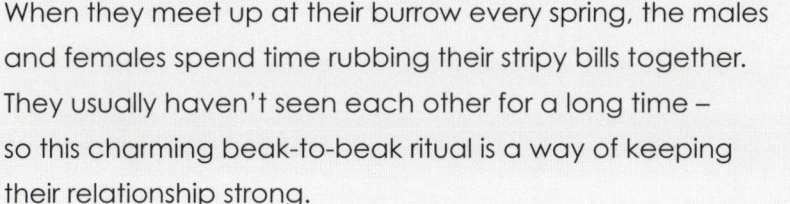

Puffins often catch more than a hundred sand eels a day – sometimes grabbing dozens at a time – so it's terrible for the birds if there are no eels to be found. One of the effects of climate change is that there are fewer sand eels, which also means fewer puffins. **It shows us why it's so important for nature to stay balanced.**

To make a burrow for the first time, the male puffin digs a hole in the clifftop soil with its bill and feet, then lines it with grass and feathers for the female. But some puffins simply settle down in old rabbit holes – far less work!

Vampire bats live in murky caves and hollow trees, hanging upside down to sleep during the day. And when darkness falls? They flitter out to the fields to drink blood from animals such as cows and horses. Even though they might sound scary, these thumb-sized bats are incredible creatures. They live in family colonies of 100 or more and have learnt how to look after each other.

A CLOUD of BATS
rustling through the skies . . .

Vampire bats are very good at sharing. If a bat stays in the colony, another bat uses a mouth-to-mouth 'kiss' to share its last meal. This is also a way of strengthening their friendships. Vampire bats also keep each other's bodies clean, and like to roost near the bats they feel closest to.

Other species of bat, such as the banana bat, help pollinate fruits like – you've guessed it – bananas!

When females are pregnant, they roost together in a **nursery colony** for warmth and safety. They also like to keep their babies close – newborn vampire bats hold tightly to their mothers, even when the adults are in flight.

The bats' bloodthirsty diet could benefit humans in the future. When vampire bats feed from an animal, their spit contains something called draculin (named after Dracula!), which stops blood from gushing out of the wound. Doctors have experimented to see if draculin can help in human medicine.

It might sound batty, but vampire bats know how to socially distance! Bats that become sick keep themselves apart from the other healthy bats as a way of protecting the rest of the colony.

A sky-howling PACK of WOLVES . . .

These **Iberian wolves** are at the top of their food chain, moving like shadows through the mountains of Spain and Portugal. They pounce on their prey in a blur of jaws, claws and teeth, using their strength and speed to bring down wild goats, deer and other animals.

Compared to humans, wolves have superpower senses. Their hearing is around 16 times better than ours, and their sense of smell is 100 times stronger!

Every pack has one dominant male and female that have cubs together. When the cubs are born, the mother stays with them while the father and the rest of the pack find food for them to eat.

For wolves, teamwork is everything. Every pack is different – some have just two members, others more than 12 – but they all do things the wolf way. They hunt together, run together, feed together and raise cubs together. This tight-knit family works to protect its territory from other wolfpacks – and you might even hear them howling as a group. Some experts think they do this to make their family relationship stronger.

Wolves are excellent hunters, and here in Spain they find lots of **wild boar** to feed on. This is bad news for the boar, but good news for rare, ground-nesting birds called **capercaillies**. When there are too many wild boar in this area, they gobble up the birds' eggs before they've hatched, so by hunting the boar, the wolves are also helping the capercaillies.

Older male wild boar usually live alone, but females and youngsters live in big family groups of up to 50, grunting and squeaking to communicate with each other.

A fabulous *flamboyance* of FLAMINGOS ...

Flashy flocks of more than a thousand **flamingos** live here in the Bahamas, where the waters are shallow and salty. These bright pink armies are fussy about their food. They bend their S-shaped necks and dip their big beaks below the water's surface to feed on **shrimp**, **algae** and **larvae** – all of which contain the red-orange colour that turns the flamingos' feathers pink.

One reason that flamingos live in such large flocks is for safety. While some birds snack on shrimp, others keep a beady eye out for predators, honking loudly to warn their pink friends.

Once a year, these flamboyant birds build chimney-shaped nests out of mud, using their webbed feet to mould it into shape. They like making nests very close to each other, turning the shoreline into a kind of muddy flamingo campsite. A single egg is laid, then protected by both parents.

When the chicks are born, the whole community comes together to look after them. Grown-ups gather the baby birds into groups known as **crèches**. A small number of adults then stay with the chicks, babysitting them while the other parents flap away to find food. Flamingo chicks are born grey, but their fluffy feathers gradually turn rosy pink as they eat more.

Flamingo parents have an unusual way of feeding their chicks. Both the mothers and fathers can produce a dark-red liquid, known as crop milk, from deep inside their throats, which they dribble into the beaks of their babies.

55

In North America, this **evergreen forest** stands over another of our natural wonders: a **freshwater river**. Waterways like this are vital for plants and animals – so where you find a river, you'll find life! **Rivers are magnets for biodiversity.**

This busy **beaver** family likes chomping on roots and river weeds. If a beaver senses danger, it slaps its tail on the water to warn the others. Beavers are brilliantly adapted to this environment – they have waterproof fur, and their babies, called **kits**, can swim just hours after being born.

Roaming the river, a run of SALMON...

Salmon spend their lives in water – but, perhaps surprisingly, they support the trees around them, too. Scientists have discovered that rivers with lots of salmon also have lots of trees growing along the banks. This is because most salmon die after laying their eggs, and their bodies contain vital nitrogen that gets soaked up by the riverbanks, which helps nearby trees to grow.

And it's not just trees that benefit. These regal **bald eagles** are on the lookout for salmon, too. The birds are at the top of the river food chain, and without fish to eat they'd go hungry.

Evergreen trees such as **pines** and **redwoods** keep their green needles year round. This gives birds and other animals a place to shelter in winter – all of which helps to keep biodiversity in balance.

Salmon take their family duties super-seriously. These silvery fish are born in mountain rivers, then swim huge distances downstream to the ocean. Years later, when it's time to become parents, they struggle all the way back upstream – laying their eggs in the exact place where they were born.

A deep-rooted grove of TREES...

Trees keep us alive. They make food from water, sunlight and carbon dioxide, then release oxygen, which humans and animals need to breathe. Our planet has trillions of trees, from mighty **oaks** and gentle **willows** to giant **firs** and ancient **yews**. And as well as helping us, they also help each other . . .

In a forest, every tree looks as though it's growing separately, but there's magic happening below the ground. Each tree has thick roots that twist through the soil, collecting water to send up the trunk and into the branches. Attached to the roots are thin strands of **fungi**, which spread out to reach the roots of other trees, forming a huge underground web, connecting tree to tree.

Trees can use this maze-like network of roots and fungi to 'talk' to each other, sending messages and sharing important nutrients. This extraordinary marvel of nature is taking place right beneath your feet! It means older trees can pass sugars and water to younger trees, helping them grow, while trees threatened by disease are able to warn their neighbours.

Our trees provide a home for some of our most amazing insects, birds and reptiles.

Trees can even communicate with animals. Some elms, for example, release a special smell when their leaves are being chewed by **caterpillars** – and the smell attracts caterpillar-eating **wasps**!

Here in this European forest, many mammals need trees, too: **squirrels** scamper up them, **dormice** doze in them and **badgers** burrow under them.

Clever **oaks** and **beeches** have a special trick for creating future generations of trees. Every five to ten years they have 'mast years', when they produce far more **acorns** and **nuts** than normal. Because the woodland wildlife can't eat them all, it means some will survive and become new trees.

A bustling CROWD of HUMANS

Humans are amazing. We show love, compassion and kindness. We cross seas, climb mountains and build bridges. Because humans live in so many different countries and have so many different values and family structures, it's sometimes easy to forget how much we all have in common. We all have hopes, fears and friendships. We all tell stories, make plans and share ideas. We're one species, living together on one planet.

The impact that humans have on the natural world is huge.
Human-made problems like deforestation, pollution, and climate change are very bad news for biodiversity – but we also have the power to change things for the better.

In a world without biodiversity, it would be impossible for us to live normally. The air we breathe, the food we eat and the water we drink all come from nature. **Nature needs our protection** – but that's just one side of the story. **We need nature to protect us, too.**

Every single one of us lives close to nature. Even in busy cities, we're never far away from wildlife and outdoor spaces. We see birds in the sky, trees along the streets and insects in the soil. Just like us, all these things are vital pieces in the great jigsaw of life. We all have our place in one wild family, and we all have this one planet to share.

We humans have a special ability to help other living things. Today there are nearly eight billion humans, and every single one of us can influence the world that we live in. By the actions we take and the choices we make, we can help our wild biodiverse family to stay strong.

Everything in our world is carefully connected.

Everything that swims, walks or flies. Everything that flowers, hatches or grows. Life on our planet has spent billions of years evolving, and we've been left with a shared home that's too valuable for words.

Every living thing has a part to play in life on Earth. From the creepy-crawlies that are so vital to nature's food chains, and the mammals that bind our ecosystems together, to the birds that nest in the bushes, and the trees that create our mighty forests.

For biodiversity, the future can sometimes look scary. Some of our actions as humans can be very harmful to the natural world – but it's not too late to change the tale. One of the things we've learned is that when nature is given the chance, it knows how to bounce back.

We've met families of all shapes and sizes in these pages. Some live in the great blue of the ocean. Others live in the dense green of the rainforest. Others live in the dark brown of the soil. Our world is home to endless incredible species – all of them, and all of us, are part of . . .

For Daisy Florence Williams, with love – B.L.

For the families that find you – H.H.

PUFFIN BOOKS

UK | USA | Canada | Ireland | Australia | India | New Zealand | South Africa

Puffin Books is part of the Penguin Random House group of companies
whose addresses can be found at global.penguinrandomhouse.com.

www.penguin.co.uk   www.puffin.co.uk   www.ladybird.co.uk

Penguin
Random House
UK

First published 2023
001

Printed in China
The authorized representative in the EEA is Penguin Random House Ireland,
Morrison Chambers, 32 Nassau Street, Dublin D02 YH68
A CIP catalogue record for this book is available from the British Library
ISBN: 978–0–241–51493–1

All correspondence to: Puffin Books, Penguin Random House Children's,
One Embassy Gardens, 8 Viaduct Gardens, London SW11 7BW

FSC
www.fsc.org

MIX
Paper from
responsible sources
FSC® C018179